Eleven Yellow Jerseys

Karen Press

Illustrated by Elizabeth Pulles

Heinemann

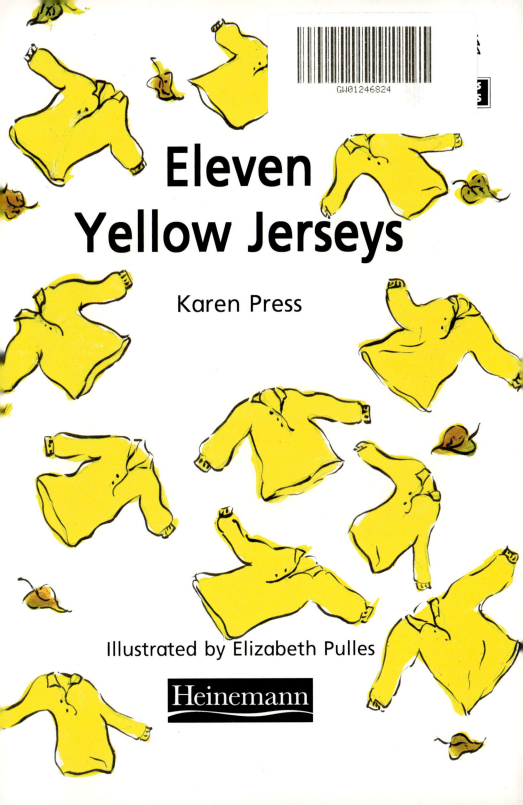

Eleven yellow jerseys are drying on the line.

It is the day of the big football match.
The players are getting ready.

'Who will win?' says Teboho.
'We will!' the players shout.
'Sunshine Team are the best!'

Fikile goes outside to fetch the jerseys.
'Help! Help!' he shouts.
'The wind has blown our jerseys away!'

The wind blows harder and harder. Soon the yellow jerseys are flying over the houses.

'Hurry!' Teboho says. 'We must catch our jerseys! Run!'

Three jerseys are stuck in the big plum tree.
Jonas finds a long stick.
He pulls the jerseys out of the tree.

Two dogs are chewing a jersey.
'Shoo! Shoo!' says Nomonde.
She chases the dogs away.

Lindiwe sees a taxi in the road.
'Stop! Stop!' she shouts.
'There is a jersey on your roof!'

'Ouch!' says Ben.
He is pulling two jerseys off
a cactus bush.

Four jerseys are floating down the river.
Dudu and Themba try to catch them.

The children go back to the house.
They have found all the jerseys.
'Now get dressed,' says Teboho.
'We are late for the match!'

The Sunshine Team has a new name.
Today they are the Muddy Team.

But they win the cup.

Activity

What happened to the jerseys in the pictures?

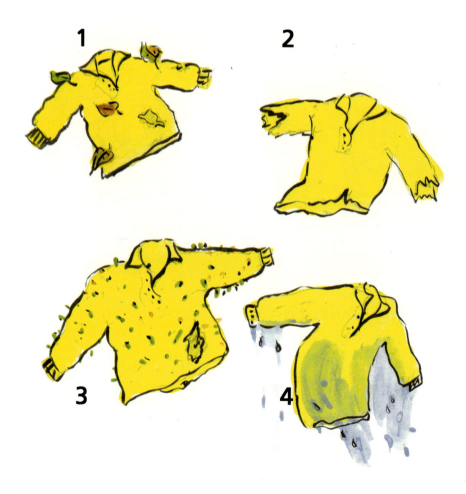